BLUE BUT NOT BROKEN

By Naoise Gale

Advance Praise for *Blue But Not Broken*

"*Blue But Not Broken* is dually a delve into the human psyche and a wider exploration of what we mean to the people around us. Trauma and tenderness are expertly laid bare and Gale's work is breathless, rooted, transcendent. It carves its own path through the themes we all think we know and shows us the burning issues that lie beneath. Raw seems an understatement when describing a collection that wounds with such excruciating, necessary purpose."

—Laura Jane Round, Black Country-born performance poet
and author of *The Coveted* (Cerasus Poetry, 2021)

"This collection from Naoise Gale is as blisteringly honest, heartbreaking at times, yet life-enhancing as her debut *After The Flood Comes The Apologies*. Yet here she digs deeper; her poetry fires and fries the synapses, her words lit by the stark fluorescent light of hospital wings and fizzing with the effervescence of pill-popped pharmaceuticals. An astonishingly mature collection from a vital new voice."

—JP Seabright, Writer, and Assistant Editor, Full House Literary

"As a sister Lost Girl, this is poetry I've been waiting for my entire life. Naoise Gale's gift for utterly original, bizarre, beautiful imagery that speaks the unspeakable is unmatched – she gives us glitter-bombed crabs; old ladies 'wearing icy perms'; the sky as 'spilt apple juice'; lightning; Catherine of Siena. But more than this – 'let's binge the distance' – these poems are an earnest and total capturing of the neurodivergent female experience in all its trauma (or 'meadows'): grief, fear, guilt, alienation, medical gaslighting, and agonising capacity for love. These poems are, admittedly, sometimes blue, but there is absolutely nothing broken about them…seldom have I read anything so whole."

—Olivia Tuck, author of
Things Only Borderlines Know (Black Rabbit Press, 2019);
Assistant Editor of Lighthouse Journal
and Tears in the Fence

Blue But Not Broken

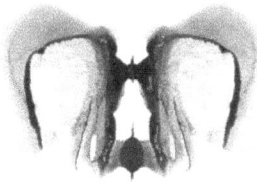

Naoise Gale

Gale, Naoise / author

Blue But Not Broken / Naoise Gale

Poems

ISBN: 979-8-9869524-6-8

Edited by: Jude Marr
Book Design: Amanda McLeod
Cover Art: morningarage via iStock
Cover Design: Amanda McLeod

PUBLISHER
Femme Salvé Books
An Imprint of Animal Heart Press
1854 Hendersonville Rd. Ste A
PMB 211
Asheville, NC 28803
www.femmesalvebooks.net
www.animalheartpress.net

For my granny,
who loves fearlessly,
regardless.

Table of Contents

IMPLODE

EXPLODE

IMPLODE

Pre-Diagnosis, an Autistic Girl Begins Disintegration

Twelve years old, I was scared
they'd touch the clock
of my clever and name it forged.

If the equation curled itself around
the bedpost, it would become
impossible — I would become

impossible. I was scared they'd
locate the fraud of me, the squiggled
stupid of my tongue, all wool

and breathless. They found it anyway,
a playdough brain I'd once cupped
in my palms. Clever doesn't

buy you anything, just fake friends
who glimmer when you fail. A mediocre
breakdown when the sun once called you

a prodigy, when the teacher tied string
to your navel and talked about getting
through it. Written permission

to die afterwards. Too many aimless
car journeys, empty-skulled.
Your brain somewhere

on the motorway, growling at Ferraris.
Melting in the rain. Has anyone seen a brain?
This specific brain, miss, I have no desire

for your brain, mine is special,
it may kill me. I am looking for it
in a lukewarm Ensure. A steri-strip.

A patch emitting fuzzy and fine.
A couple hundred nurses with rough
thumbs. A cannula, a bottle of Feroglobin.
A mother stringing up fairy lights.

Separation Anxiety Disorder

having some weird row about ice cream flavours
glitter bombing a crab at the beach forking feta
baked in oil and mint dabbing on orange eyeshadow
asking if my periods will start soon burying my bra
and my phone and my polar bear toy not eating
the yoghurt with almonds and honey singing a sad song
at the stars writing down the same honest cliché
or swimming my pot-belly slim trying to drown myself
counting each kiss my mother left on my fingers like one
clawing at my father two slashing my thighs on sea-rock
three texting on the toilet four smelling sweat everywhere
like eww like five waking up dazed and empty
six lobbing boats at the windows seven
stalking a black cat down the road to the airport
eight sicking up a baguette gulping seawater nine walking
through red dust and lawyers threatening to run away
whispering *I'm ten years old*
ten years old like that meant more than a pebble or a fish
or a rope of seaweed wishing myself rich and adult wishing
myself out of petrol stink and sand and scratching my arms
to pus and silent motorway journeys re-emerging at two am
spooned by my mother saying
I missed you I missed you I missed you x

The Pharmacy Trembles With Knowing

It may well be that it's Saturday morning and Granny is threatening
my hair into a floppy pony. Mum works eight till eight with no gaps
then appears at the door to hug me soft as a dishcloth. She smells of
resin and money, her hair dark and glossy as a dream, sprayed over

shoulders. Pale light dances across cottage slats. The sun is out but
it's cold and damp and the up-and-coming village is still coming up;
Southern tourists pronounce *Slawit* sloppily, the name pantomimed
in their monied mouths. Brunches haven't yet been invented

but we cross fairyland woods purpled with berries to the canal where
Granny once witnessed a body being buried. On picnic benches,
crisps and nettles, but not today. Instead, a cafeteria on a narrow
boat. This is Yorkshire countryside rewritten by studio execs. Our

sky wears a flat cap. Our chairs face the edge of silent green water.
I'm slapped with factor fifty — or perhaps it's raining. The village
red and oozing sludge from storm drains. Sometimes, it floods.
We sit inside as a three: me and Granny across from Mum.

The pharmacy is algae-green through our circular windows,
glossed as a beetle, close enough to nick a fingertip of cream.
Crumpets with honey butter. A tall coke float. The pharmacy
is curious of our rituals, perhaps a little afraid of what it all means.

Closeness. Someone shrugs a fleece onto my arms. I'm watching
this scene and I'm watching the pharmacy watching me and
I'm scared of what it all means. Clasping tight as a promise,
Granny whistles *Hushabye Mountain* down my ears, kisses

my nose, mimes an agnostic *God Bless*. One day my friend will die
and I'll sing *a gentle breeze* across his improvised wake — I'll remember
him watching me, violets burning up in his eyes, *you have a lovely voice.*
I want to kiss someone for no reason. We're still gentle. *Close your eyes.*

Kissing

Purple-haired boy from the chicken shop tugs me outside to
stars
and rain, to cat-eye-bleached puddles and breath that
smells
of oil, gunpowder. The moon is a sliver. We catch silvery
droplets
on tongues then kiss soft as spiderwebs, all petrichor. I'm in fleece
pyjamas
and his hands hold my waist like a violin.
Thumbs
and buttons and stars. A shock of tongue. Thumbs; buttons;
stars.

LIGHTNING NEVER FORKS MY THIGHS TO HEAVENS.

A "Gifted" Child's Guide to Accelerating Burnout

Eleven star corpses tacked on frail crepe paper
brush bruises from lips and tap blood from gnawed thumbs.
With daydreams of poisoned porcupine punctures,
girl shreds certificate, fevers.

Step one: love it. Tickle prospectuses and carve
formulae into kneecaps. Applaud fragmentation.
Graze infinite extracurriculars and vision-board
eleven star corpses tacked on frail crepe paper.

Step two: memorise everything. Goggles; smoke;
the taste of rotting. Prove everybody wrong
and make it by sixteen. Quit life and hope hollow grades
brush bruises from lips and tap blood from gnawed thumbs.

Step three: loathe it. Anchor arms with ice packs and watch
your skin get soggy. Argue that it isn't self-harm. Argue
with no one in particular — find order in numbers then lose it
with daydreams of poisoned porcupine punctures.

Step four: forget everything. Mug cakes; log flumes;
the blaze of winning. Prove nobody wrong
and fall apart by eighteen. Scatter blame like confetti. Marry
tragedy. Shred certificate, fever.

Mirror Girls

Before we were fat or thin,
before snakeskin armouries
and comrades crippled
by wanting, we degraded
our bodies together, slipped
laughter between furtive
desks, made our mouths
an echo: *you're so perfect,*
my thighs are gross, I wish
I had your body, this stomach,
do you see these rolls? Each
shaking skin like maracas,
each drooling over bones
and mascara, over figures
that shadowed the hallways
and made us mean. All tempted
by erasure, not just of the body
but of something bigger,
the needy part
that threw ponchos atop miniskirts
in frigid winter, that confessed
sexualities on teenaged
sleepovers and, once, touched
something brighter than hunger.
The part that drove us anaesthetised
into alien cupboards and made
self-annihilation from our hands.
The part we called womanhood,
tossing cloned heads and foraging
for kisses, or girlhood, or maybe
a set of experiences shared

between five or six who didn't
hear the music when they danced.
When I got fat, they withdrew
from self-deprecation, wailed
that my body was fine; that
was how I knew it wasn't.
When I got thin, they gloated
over a scaffolding of bones,
whispered odes then begged
me to stop. They knelt before
the skeletal messiah of a girl
they once knew, beckoned
for a mirror, and pretended
that they hadn't been praying
for the exact same insanity.

Anorexia

i.
made my life a lesson
in subtraction, two negatives
touching wrists to birth
a girl, hairless.

Inside her was a thin, grey dagger
buried in feathers.
The tip protruded like a cod's
head, writhing. It never
drew blood of any colour.
Legend says the dagger-fish gobbled
the bird, though my bird still knew
flight. The girl

(let's binge the distance — I am the girl)

plucked the feathers one
by one and picked small,
snapped bones from my
teeth. I enshrined a nest
for ghosts then one morning
lost it. And the high was cold as
cream, unwhipped.

ii.
February coughed and
everything fuzzed. Vision
popped like a fisheye
on *I'm a celeb*. You can

taste a blackout before it
arrives, sour and metallic,
but you can't scare it away
with feathers or knives.
The doctor told me to
lick a spanner

for the anaemia; my
fist became the heaviest
and loveliest thing about me.
She kissed granite and bone
Like *I. Love. You.* Remembered
anger in threes, all blunt
physicalities and screaming.

iii.
Moths get everywhere but
they prefer the throat. Felt
plugged my mouth and some bitch
shovelled all that snow from
my stomach which is just a
metaphor to say that it
hurt, badly and intermittently,

and when it didn't hurt
I scratched up my face
and begged forgiveness,
and when forgiveness
never came I knew I
didn't deserve it.

iv.
I am hunting for
God in a nasogastric
tube because the word
Light sounds frail
and sad and holy.

v.
Since we're speaking in
apocalypses, I would rather be
a dagger than
a fish
or a moth
or a dead bird
or a scrap of felt
or a woman
or all these stricken,
shaking feathers.

Marshmallows

Yesterday, I bought marshmallows at the corner shop.
The sky was spilled apple juice, and the day
was closer than ants. At the till, bearded
man asked:

"Is your head screwed on right yet?"

as though I was shampoo cap or faulty tyre,
as though I didn't know the pain of unbleeding.
You were every meaty man on a motorbike.
Paranoid, I skipped double-yellows and
crossed each zebra twice.

I didn't tell beard-man about the sweetness
of marshmallows as they re-emerge, nude,
or the way they float like candy rubber
ducks in the sick-splashed bowl.

A man in leathers entered and I hid behind
the carnation milk. I did not want
to be seen purchasing such sin
on a Sunday.

Catherine of Siena, Sainted Anorexic, on Her Starving Rituals

My angels and devils get muddled up. Swap
shoulders sometimes, hold hands hostage
in hellfire prayer. Have you seen the little minx

with the god-white teeth and the crewcut?
She told me I could eat as many satsumas
as I wanted; she birthed my mouth and I sucked that juice

like the blessed starved. She stroked my lips
when I whimpered, sold flesh for pennies. Played a disco tune
on repeat. We spun golden in the morning;

when it got sad she rocked me to sleep. And her pal —
geez! Those brimstone eyes. Matte black lipstick
and a flimsy red dress. I guess I like her style. Every so often

she mirages a new reflection in my mirror,
paints me something small and strong. Un-staples
my tongue and tempts words to fill the void.

Miss God! She has been waiting so long! Her hair
is falling out! Her smile is blue and broken! Sometimes
I think they are in it together. I imagine them

breeding in my chest. Look here — so many
imperfect daughters. All of us stricken and seething.
All of us guilty and grateful. They hate-fucked me to life

and now they are cumming
all over my heart. I wish they would quiet down.
I wish they would thicken the walls. All these multitudes
hurt me too much. I think I hunger. I thank Heavens.

The Pharmacy Asks If I'm Hungry

Sometimes there's simply nothing left to eat. Microwaved cod
glistens like a thin sheet of marble. I move my paper-plate paws
through whiskey glasses trembling with coppers — the pharmacy
slumps against the bank's giant green pillars, a hungry addict.

It's another yellow day with Lily and her dirty tricycle. Kitten-milk
men smile from al-fresco pubs, their mouths split open like tins of
sardines, their lust netted lemons, hanging, in jeans. The pharmacy
ogles my flimsy supermarket carrier, my tiny body, hauling bottles.

Monica smokes the room and talks of her cat's diabetes — I say *mi
dispiace* and unwrap another Baci truffle, shivering the foil. The new
café is good, apparently, sells hot chocolate thick as custard; the
pharmacy is jealous, huddles in wooden puddles with medicinal tea.

I have stopped visiting my granny for fear of orange macaroni on
blue chipped china. I have stopped eating for fear of my stomach
puffing up like popcorn. Downtown, old ladies stop at the pharmacy
to collect Pepto Bismol, heart medication, or to gossip with other

old ladies wearing icy perms and chalk tongues. I'm seventeen,
ghosting cross town in my sixties diamond mini, eliciting thin music:
whistles; gasps; the occasional smashed glass. The pharmacy
offers coffee-n-walnut, chocolate tiffin, weak mocha, and observes

my tap-shoe strut across slow cobbles to bus station, where I buy
the blissful inedible: flapjacks with ginger; shiny cola sweets;
Pringles stacked up like ammunition. The pharmacy
is a kind young man who wants to feed me slices of pizza, on

a bust-up single, with his hand up my top. The pharmacy glitters
with sympathy and syrup-weak codeine. The pharmacy sirens Bowie
on speakers that cut up summer into brittle poetry, the pharmacy
says *Ziggy* says *strung out* says *lasers* the pharmacy cups my face,
dog's dinner silver, and says: love, *you better hang on to yourself.*

Thread

Mercurial autumn day. Rain pounding
the ground, sound of cicadas. Pearls
of pills in the palm of a girl who doesn't
know what she's doing. Slosh of water
on the sill. Sound of drowning. She funnels
them into her mouth, sickly baby bird,
nightingale foetus. Waits. The rain drizzles
silver as pewter. The clouds Viennese waltz.
She sinks mallow-soft into her sheets. Stunned
eyes. Hiccupy breaths. Sweet, stoned chest.
Who could have guessed what would happen
next? Who could have guessed?

EXPLODE

Confession

I bleed *down there* most days
because I took too much Ibuprofen.

My liver is scarred with Paracetamol.

Everything inside is hospital-band blue
and quivering.

I am eighteen years old.
I ache.

Two summers ago, they warned of death by malnutrition.
I ate myself in wafers.

Forged religions in bathrooms.
Scattered scars across my arms.
Bled from every orifice, in public.

Took a taxi to the hospital
and fended off curious octogenarians.
Nearly got locked up.
Convinced eating disorder services to take me back.

It was all too much like a bad break up.
It was all too much like a good breakdown.

Now I am obese and people
treat me like cheap cereal.

The only thing left is the codeine.
Perfect and hollow.
Sweet and potent.
A love bucket.
A weather of nausea.

Nothing much to worry about.
I die by degrees.

The Night He Prescribed You

I laid in bed with moths squabbling
in the darkness and bit my tongue
until blood pooled in a deep, velvety gash.
The room was black as imminent collapse.
My ears buzzed like chainsaws. I was so high

I could feel my chest rising and falling
like the bubbles of a lava lamp. I crept down
the mirrorless staircase and felt the image
of myself liquify and drip down the walls,

knife-fight gunge. You hissed from the open
bottle. I wanted to swallow you in one protracted
gulp, dark as wine,
smooth as silvery spider-down.
I wanted to feel the thorn
of your fingernails on my neck. I wanted

to die for you. You were a phallic bulge
in my pocket when the lights came on,
when the screaming started.

My mother was ghoulish and stupid
in the doorway —
the open drawer was fresh evidence.

You whispered in my pocket, so
I funnelled you through my palm
and covered you in hasty kisses.

Next morning was a shrill affair.

Hospital-bright. The woman in the bed
next to mine had breath
like gravestones in the rain.
When she spoke, her teeth rattled.

I read the *Get Well Soon* cards
and no one mentioned the word *thief*.

The Doctor

is a very nice man. He has your best interests at heart. The Doctor studied for thirty years to skilfully assess your pain and blame it on your womanly oddities today. The Doctor was top of his class. The Doctor took fifteen GCSEs and was featured in the local newspaper for his star-studded grades. The Doctor cares about you. He won't prescribe medication because he is concerned you will abuse it, or forgot to take it, or sell it for a thousand euros on the dark web, not because he can't be bothered to look for his pen.

The Doctor feels your pain. He feels the knitting needle lodged in your lower back. He feels the deep twisting in your ovaries. When you pass out after standing up too fast on the sweaty carriage, and wake up tumoured by concerned citizens who won't let you leave, and therefore miss your stop, he does too — he rides all the way to Mosley cross-legged on the gritty lino with his vision dark as a tunnel. When you nearly stab your mother in an episode of psychosis after six months of telephone appointments begging for some pills, he actually kills his own mother, right through the stomach with a shaky kitchen knife, and he doesn't scream afterwards either, just quietly arranges her arms to a peaceful cross in the funeral home.

The Doctor wants you to know he understands. Once, he had high blood pressure, he was four pounds overweight and eating too many takeaways, so he took up cycling and got a prescription for blood-pressure-medication from another Doctor the next day. The Doctor is an excellent typist. Your name is spelt incorrectly on purpose. Your list of diagnoses is wrong on purpose — this is actually your new list of diagnoses, bipolar is out, very twenty-ten, and The Doctor thinks you are probably *one of those hysterical personality disorder girls.*

The Doctor senses you are a hypochondriac from the moment you walk into the room with your big tits and nervous twitchy fingers threaded through your bag straps. The Doctor won't accept abuse from you. The Doctor would never ever abuse the nurses. The Doctor doesn't believe in chronic pain, endometriosis, POTS, or autism in women. The Doctor thinks you need a new hobby. The Doctor thinks you should try eating salad in the sunshine, drinking your tall water with a little paper umbrella, and eliminating all sources of stress from your life. The Doctor sleeps eight hours a night and doesn't own a television. The Doctor is privately educated. The Doctor grew up in a detached house in suburbia and enjoyed skiing trips to Switzerland in the holidays. The Doctor has never visited a council estate. The Doctor loves his wife. The Doctor has a BMI of twenty-two. The Doctor finds chocolate *too sweet*.

If you haven't met The Doctor yet, you will: he will suggest Cognitive Behavioural Therapy for your bladder infection, citalopram for your thrush, desogestrel for your manic episodes, and when you're not looking, he will write HYPOCHONDRIAC in your medical notes, so when you next ask for help you will never again see anyone except The Doctor, armed with a bottle of multivitamins and a *can-do* attitude and the sunny certainty that there is still nothing wrong with you.

I'm Not Very Good at Being Depressed

My therapist says I am a victim
of coercive control I say
I am one rough look away
from an overdose.
And I am not bipolar I am
moonlight. And I am not
trauma I am meadows.
I am autism, but only
when it rains, which
is always, thank fuck.
And I am not BPD
because the doctors
never wrote it down,
or they wouldn't admit to it.
And I scrawled skylines
all over my thighs
to hurt something solid,
and I pressed my guts
into a bottle top
to shiver with the gold
of an energy drink,
to become a door
and a lock and a locked
door. And when I was
eleven I tried to break
my wrist by flying-falling,
or by hammer, but
something always stopped me
like a spoon balanced
on the end of my nose or the trace
of some dead twin crawling up

my spine, so I mashed it
with a hairbrush instead,
until it was blue
but not broken.
And none of this
is poetry. And when
the pills hit I go green
and godly and I feel
like a beer bottle
in the strobe lights
on some ugly man's lips,
and the nausea is everything
I love all at once. And none
of this is poetry. And I am
just some fat chick
begging you to call
me clever and my hands
are whittling all
these pebbles to bone.
And I am singing
to myself. And none of this
is poetry.

Apology to My Mother

Every time we fight
you sweep up the glass, rehang
certificates to prove
I am not mould or dust.

I hate that you love me as much when I blister
as when I melt to wax and dark and sad
as when I am a star scorching the night to ash.
I hate that last week I hit myself
over the head
with a torch and afterwards
you held me like a precious, precious stone.

You say I want to be punished
like a Victorian. When things get loud
I cover my ears and think
of death till the sense fuses.
When the concussion-fuzz
fades I kiss my brain
at all its broken corners.

The word *odd* burns
at the splinter-edge of vision.

I Hate You for Asking / The Answer is Yes

I reclined on the red leather sofa,

> cheeks pink and round as helium balloons,
> pupils shrinking into bloom,
> skin humming with pleasure.

You asked if I was high
and my breath caught in my throat
like I'd swallowed a locket, like you were
dragging chainmail out of my gullet;

> I hissed *no* like something evil
> and fixed my papery eyes
> on the opiate fuzz of the television screen.
> The lies fell soft as cherry blossom

and crackled, ruby sparks in the hearth.
The truth curled beside
your warm, forgiving arms. It panted

> as my chest rose and fell
> like a doomed civilisation and something
> soft squirmed beneath my sternum;

a key twitched between the hollow bones
and made music, as though I was a body
and an instrument, nothing more. The pills

> clattered like broken crockery
> in my stomach, which was red as bloody
> sunsets and churning with acid.

The moment passed and the high ached
in my throat and your bruised smile was
like a splinter I couldn't remove.

The Pharmacy Worries About Me

Realistically, I'm impractical to love. Who would love my life
of regimented chocolate from the corner shop, moonlit binges, new
money, grass verges beyond a boyfriend's car, his waist burnt up
like a fever? I appreciate no-questions-asked pharmacies with fibrous

green laxatives. My five-year plan stipulates that this love will be long
as a pantomime: soon I'll appreciate no-questions-asked pharmacies
with surplus opiates, minimal foresight, nothing like
the pharmacy who clocked my Sherlockian disguise (dungarees

and a big hat) and said in a tall voice *I can't sell you this every week* —
I was a bashful tit, swallowed whole by the parody of my frog hat.
But now I'm eighteen. Late for a shift at McDonalds' — my trousers
are too tight and I keep calling in sick. I'm gentle. An easy muse.

Avoiding the tongue of a boy who dyed his hair purple for me. Little
does he know, I prefer blue. He picks me up in his fast red car, shiny
as leather. He drives me to Leeds with the roof down and *Fireflies*
pounding round the rubber like breeze. I neither talk nor kiss just

simper in my breasts then breathe onto his neck and he ejaculates.
He knows my cropped black jumper and frilly black skirt and cold
eyelashes on the motorway, but the pharmacy knows the fixed eye
underneath — my dread of angry managers, sucked nipples, long

college days clammy with calories. I buy miniature Stroopwafels,
sneak-eat them on the bus, hands combing through canvas bag,
pig subtle. The pharmacy knows my stretched white skin, ripped
at the hips and bust, scarred kintsugi from when the hunger returned.

The pharmacy knows me as bulimic baby chewing Malted Milks
in the attic, huddled over the bucket while hail thrashes the roof.
The pharmacy knows purge-slimy fingers, my grubby habits, frogged
focaccia caught in the throat, the salve of still-cold ice cream,

the incontinent climax; the pharmacy offers anaesthesia regardless.
It touches my throat, acid-sore, laughs: *please put down your hands.*

I Like Myself When I'm High

It was spring: dotted flowers, candyfloss
horizons. Cherry blossom trees that
twirled into pastel skies and stood silhouetted
in the pale dawn light. Pink, nubile trees in
bud, making the ground a rosy desiccated
shore, flute song. Skeins of thin, translucent
rain. I laid in the grass, danced my hands around
my flushed face, swiped them across my doped
mouth, made shadow puppets on the lit
bark. It was a cucumber fresh day, breezy.
My pills scattered like white, weeping apple blossom
in the dark crevice of my handbag. I twitched
my hands around the space, pressed six
pills onto my tongue and swallowed
with perennial bottled water. The geese kept a-
bobbing. The blossom never shuddered.
My heart sang *I love you I love you I love you*
like a ruddy puncture, slow pumping, reggae
music where mothers go to die.
Tolerance kept me a neutral angel, nourished
by whiteness, lungs a slow approximation
of spring loving. Later, I dozed by the lake — sickly
jasmine slumber — while the sweet
wind stripped the trees and the bubble-gum
blossom buried me deeper, deeper, deeper.

Dating a Neurotypical

1

Why do we whisper
in bars while the sun nods and
glow-worms wriggle across clouds?

Because halloumi
and wine, aphrodisiac
lightbulbs and remote break-ups.

2

Why no misty trace
of finger on forearm? Why
all ice, your gaze a ghost ship?

To touch eyes would be
to die burning, cobalt blue.
All that space is electric.

3

Why must our night-sweats
mate in the virgin dark? Why
no skies, streetlamps or mercy?

Because cumming and
stars. Love howling at the moon.
Some sad dust dies when we touch.

My dear, why so much
dark before daybreak? Why so
few texts, so much horizon?

No horizon, no
daybreak; no silence, no sun;
no glow-worms, no dark, no us.

Scorched May

Gone the insipid green
of April, the powdered skies
and buds that stink
of too much attention, the easy
dew wetting barefoot princesses.
No — Spring wears
a sixties mini, drives a Fiat.
Changing meadows and bubblemint
vistas. A lone skylark on a sapless
branch. Peonies upon peonies.
A whole field of them — vape
smoke. Tang of cherries
on a crude tongue. Perhaps
Spring had whispered to Summer,
told her to burst into bud, the girl
needs help, needs a crackle of heat.
The girl needs to sink in pubescent
hay, needs chilli chocolate
and alchemy, needs cockle lips
and *Modern Muse* by Estée Lauder.
Needs daisies, needs moonshine.
Needs and never returns, little
library lifter. Needs and never
apologies. Disingenuous weeping
willow tears on cracked benches.
Cat-scratched arms and pills
in secret hiding places. Peonies
upon peonies upon peonies.

So Ink Your Eyes

Mist bandaged Venice
like a mother. Stemmed
arteries first, then skin.
Coils of smoke mushroomed
from Vaporetti, water frayed
at the hulls and you died
quiet in another city. It wasn't snowing.
The air had no unusual bite.
The egret tight-roped along splitting
black cord. The heron speared
tiny, glinting fish that thrived
in half-clear, half-murky
water. You wrote and deleted
an iMessage. You gripped a blade,
trembling or steady, I'm not sure.
The sun slept
under marshy covers. The rain
named it comatose. Saltwater
spilled onto pavements, forced
people into boots and duffel
coats. They wrote eulogies
in the condensation. They trudged
mud through supermarkets,
bought an octopus
from the freezer aisle. I watched
the city sink. I wanted to lift it up
with my thumbs; I wanted
to kiss it into hell.

One Every Four Days

I think I was on the train when you slit your wrists. Listening
to Radiohead, musing melancholy, oblivious to the rivulets of blood,
the last-minute doubts, the deleted texts. I had seen you the day
before, a smiling pixelated face. We were going to dance the Time
Warp. I don't know if I loved you, but you made me feel human.
Sexy thing, all legs. Nineteen. Dynamite.

They resurrected your ghost on Halloween, no kidding. Devils
laughed and vomited into buckets. So many bones, very little flesh.
I like to think of you wearing your Belstaff, quietly dead and
meringue stiff, white and unbloodied. Who am I kidding? Your final
violence ploughed into my stomach and left me mangled origami.
Some wretched parade of grief. Unjustified, I felt, a mute drifting
friend, no messages between us. Too distant for that last honour roll
— you named who mattered and who didn't. That night, I sent my
mother back to England and binged to remind myself I was alive.
Even the pointless stars were daggers. The toilet glared in their
pharmaceutical light.

After the snot and the ferrous rage, after so many gluttonous, jerking
afternoons, I stopped feeling your loss. I watched documentaries on
suicide dry-eyed. I forgot the myriad damage and tied a half-hearted
noose around my own neck, called it contagious. The family hated us
for unknown reasons, and the uni tossed your name into a scrapheap
of other lost, delusional souls. Worked too hard, didn't work hard
enough, insufficient even in death. They erased the word suicide and
murmured very sad, what a waste. Rang at risk students, two-minute
phone call, then silence. We sang vigils for you in cluttered bedrooms.
Unlearned tears and grew babies in undisturbed wombs. Forgot
how to love you. None of us thought of waste, or potential, or future.
You were here and then you were gone.

You blazed and we didn't care if you made it or not. Rather a third than a corpse. Rather a drop-out than a corpse. The anorexic withered and pressed pictures of you. We loved you.

We loved you.

Rewriting Your Epitaph Three Times

The ladybird shines candy-apple for defence.
You were laughter that didn't break. Cellos.
Indie jumpers and feathers in your hair.
I chip off the gloss and you are wax-white,
a ghost trembling. A fury of eyes by the lake.

(Most beetles live a single year.)

The night they told me I vomited
and sent my mother home. Three-
hundred sixty-four more nights clutching
ceramic and spitting neon bile
into dark, watery nothing. The lifespan
of a glitter-bug just grieving
in the damp.

(Fireflies glow bright to communicate.)

All we saw was glory, mute.
Our hard, blank bodies swarming to light,
circling a spent, throbbing sun.
Your gorgeous flare a dowry and an arson.

(Some male spiders just want to be eaten.)

Our Love Lies

In a field full of thistles, velvet-
smooth and crushed by the weight
of a thunderous mauve sky. Lightning
cracks in a violet spangle, and illuminates
my grey hand clutching yours
like a dead flower, like a fallen star,
like angel dust and porcelain. I look into
your clouded eyes and wonder why
our feelings are nothing more than spilled
Ribena, why your heather lips
are parted to silent music not a bloom
of kisses, why your hand is colder
than sea frets. In truth, I never laid
next to you like this — we were separate
ghosts even prior to death, stripped
by a poltergeist wind, sanded to the skeleton
key chimes that tinkled through the lonely
night. There were no stars
on the night of your funeral. No songs.
Only family. I laid on my own in the field
full of thistles. Stared at the grandfather-clock
of the moon. And cried. Oh God,
how my tears soaked the soil. The wind
broke about me. The wind
broke about me.

Mixed Episode

Technicolour multiverse creation, I snipped
at my skin with fabric scissors, watched
the blood unspool like silk thread, clown bright.
My body denied scarring. I bled
like I was barely breathing. Listening
to *Lust for Life* and eating tinned macaroni,
I crawled under paranoid bedsheets and
kicked my legs through the night — house
rhythm. Bought co-codamol at the local
chemist and took so many I may as well
have swallowed batteries. Let my stomach
become a punk scream, all marred lining
and acid. Laid gum tacky on the floor,
mind melting into body melting into
carpet. Piled duvet atop duvet
and refused to go to lectures.
Stupid, cut-up girl. Twenty-seven-club
wannabe. Paranormal-blooded freak.
Crashing maniac. Bad thing.

Wish

I would like to lock the doors to my
lungs and breathe out all my smoke
in one shadowy breath, I would like

white roses and tramadol to numb
the garrotting, I would like to lie
coffin-ready next to your grave

with my eyes on the sun and nothing
passing above me, I would like
lanugo and ivy to overrun this

wretched body, I would like to press
my hips into one thin pill, illegal-
white, I would like to hold your hand

and say it is okay, okay, okay:
we are all broken keys.

Acknowledgments

A huge, heartfelt thanks to everyone at Femme Salvé Press, especially Jude Marr and Amanda McLeod, who have directed so much of their precious energy, talents, and time towards this book.

I also extend a massive thank you to my poetry community, who have supported and guided me through this process. In particular, thanks are owed to the incredible writers who blurbed this chapbook — JP Seabright, Laura-Jane Round, and my poetry confidant, Olivia Tuck, a singular talent whose forthcoming pamphlet, *Mistresses of Arts*, is sure to delight and startle the scene. Olivia, you are destined for beautiful things. Thank you also to my precious poet friend HLR, whose work is raw and daring and fresh — you inspire me to be bold.

Thanks are also due to the organizers of the following competitions, who have supported work from Blue But Not Broken: *Mono Poetry Prize 2021,* the *Spectrum Anthology Poetry Competition by Renard Press, Fish Poetry Prize 2021 and 2022, SaveAs Writers Poetry Competition 2021, Creative Future Writers' Award 2021, Reflex Fiction Summer 2021 Flash Fiction Competition,* and the *Magdalena Young Poets' Prize 2021.*

Some poems from this chapbook were included in an earlier pamphlet, *Implode Explode* (Beir Bua Press, 2022.) I am also grateful to the editors of the following journals in which versions of these poems have previously appeared:

"Separation Anxiety Disorder" in *Moonflake Press*

"The Night He Prescribed You," published under an earlier title "Sneak," in *Re-Side Zine*

"I Like Myself When I'm High" in *Clandestine Lit*

"One Every Four Days" in *Reflex Fiction Flash Fiction Competition Summer 2021*, and later in *Healthline Zine*

"Mixed Episode" in the *Magdalena Young Poets' Prize 2021*

"Wish" in *Serotonin*

About the Author

Naoise Gale is an autistic poet from West Yorkshire who writes about neurodivergence, mental illness, and addiction. She was first-prize winner of the Ledbury Poetry Competition 2022, runner-up in the AUB International Poetry Prize 2023, and longlisted in the Bridport Poetry Competition 2023, amongst others. Her work has appeared in various publications including Atrium, Lighthouse Journal, and Tears in the Fence. Her debut pamphlet *After the Flood Comes the Apologies* was published by Nine Pens and won third prize in the Poetry Book Awards 2023. It was described in Buzz Mag as "gritty and gorgeous." Naoise is currently studying for an MA in Creative Writing Poetry at the University of East Anglia.